CANADIAN ABORIGINAL ART AND CULTURE

The Cree

ERINN BANTING

Weigl

Published by Weigl Educational Publishers Limited
6325 10th Street SE
Calgary, Alberta T2H 2Z9

Website: www.weigl.ca

Library and Archives Canada Cataloguing in Publication

 Banting, Erinn, 1976-, author
        Cree / Erinn Banting.

(Aboriginal art & culture)
Issued in print and electronic formats.
ISBN 978-1-4872-0245-3 (bound).--ISBN 978-1-4872-0246-0 (pbk.).--
ISBN 978-1-4872-0247-7 (ebook)

        1. Cree Indians--Juvenile literature. I. Title.

E99.C88B36 2015   j971.004'97323   C2015-901044-6
                                               C2015-901045-4

Printed in the United States of America in Brainerd, Minnesota
1 2 3 4 5 6 7 8 9 19 18 17 16 15

082015
100815

Project Coordinator: Heather Kissock
Design: Terry Paulhus

Every reasonable effort has been made to trace ownership and to obtain permission to reprint copyright material. The publishers would be pleased to have any errors or omissions brought to their attention so that they may be corrected in subsequent printings.

We acknowledge the financial support of the Government of Canada through the Canada Book Fund for our publishing activities.

Weigl acknowledges Getty Images, Alamy, Shutterstock, iStock, Thinkstock, the Canadian Museum of History, and Wikipedia as its primary image suppliers for this title.

Contents

The People

The Cree are one of the largest groups of **First Nations** in Canada. They live across Canada from Quebec to Alberta. Historically, they lived in three different regions of what is now Canada. The Woods Cree lived in what is now the northern parts of Saskatchewan and Manitoba, while the Plains Cree lived in the central part of what is now Manitoba, Saskatchewan, and Alberta. The Swampy Cree were found in present-day Manitoba, Ontario, and Quebec.

The name "Cree" is believed to be a shortened version of the French word "Kristineaux." This is what the French explorers called the Cree when they first came into contact with them in the 1500s. It may come from mispronouncing Kenistenoag, a Cree family name.

CREE MAP

The traditional lands of the Cree in Canada

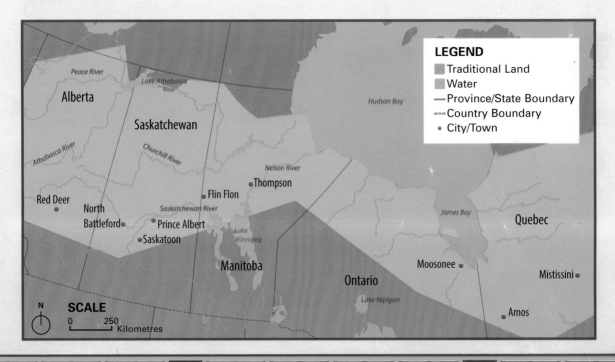

LEGEND
- Traditional Land
- Water
- — Province/State Boundary
- --- Country Boundary
- • City/Town

Peace River
Lake Athabasca
Alberta
Hudson Bay
Saskatchewan
Athabasca River
Churchill River
Nelson River
Thompson
Red Deer
Flin Flon
North Battleford
Saskatchewan River
James Bay
Quebec
Prince Albert
Lake Winnipeg
Saskatoon
Manitoba
Moosonee
Mistissini
Ontario
Lake Nipigon
Amos

N
SCALE
0   250
Kilometres

When European explorers began to arrive in the 1500s, they relied on the Cree and other Aboriginal groups for information about the country. The British and French explorers started trading with Aboriginal fur trappers, exchanging European goods for furs. The Cree soon took on the role of middlemen between the traders and the other trappers. By helping to establish the **fur trade** in this way, the Cree played an important role in the settlement of Canada.

Today, the Cree in Canada are spread out across the country, some living on **reserves** and others in cities and towns. Many Cree combine their ancient **traditions** with their daily lives in the modern world.

During the fur trade, beaver fur was valuable to both the Cree and the Europeans.

CREE WAY OF LIFE

The Cree made many items out of **birchbark**, such as **teepees** and canoes.

Cree in different regions call themselves different names, such as Nêhiyawak for Plains Cree, or Iynu for Eastern Cree.

Cree men were **excellent hunters** and **fishers**.

Cree **women** gathered plants such as **mint** for **food** and for **medicines**.

Cree Homes

Depending on the region in which they lived, the Cree had two main kinds of homes. In wooded areas, the Cree lived in birchbark homes called wigwams. On the prairies, the Cree lived in teepees, which were tents covered in bison skin. Both structures had wooden frames.

Wigwams ranged in size depending on what they were used for. Small wigwams were built as temporary shelters by hunters who followed herds of animals. Larger wigwams were built to house families and were found in Cree villages and settlements.

Teepees were useful to the Plains Cree because they were easily put up and taken down. This was important because the Plains Cree moved frequently. They followed herds of bison, caribou, elk, and moose as they **migrated** with the seasons.

Teepees are still used by the Cree during hunting season.

Wigwams were more durable than teepees and could withstand quite severe weather.

DWELLING AND DECORATION

To build a **teepee**, branches were pulled together and tied at the top to form a **cone**.

Animal hides were useful for clothing and teepees because they were warm and **waterproof.**

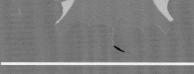

To build a **wigwam,** branches were bent into arches and tied together to form a dome.

To insulate wigwams, **moss** was added between the layers of birchbark that covered the frames.

 # Cree Communities

The Cree have a history of working and living off the land. Community is very important to the Cree because of their tradition of working together for survival. There were no rich or poor families in traditional Cree communities. Everyone in the band shared food, clothing, housing, and supplies.

To follow migrating animals, families travelled together from camp to camp. Once they chose a site, they unpacked their tools and supplies and set up their teepees. Men hunted and fished. Women typically set up camp, prepared food, cared for the children, and made clothing.

In the 1600s, there were only about 30,000 Cree in Canada. Today, there are more than 200,000.

The Cree ruled their communities based on principles of cooperation and respect for the land, their family, their beliefs, traditions, and **culture**. Cree communities were led by a person, usually a man, called a chief. In general, the chief was selected based on his bravery, generosity, and wisdom.

Today, many Cree live in permanent settlements. Advances in transportation, housing, industry, and modern conveniences have become part of Cree life. At the same time, many modern Cree still speak the Cree language and practise the traditions of their **ancestors**, including storytelling, music, and art.

Teaching children traditional Cree art forms is one way of keeping Cree culture alive.

Cree groups are still ruled by chiefs. These men or women are elected by their communities in the same way leaders are elected throughout Canada. Cree territories are ruled independently of the Canadian government. These communities have their own police forces, governments, and laws.

The Cree community of Oujé-Bougoumou was founded in 1992.

Cree Clothing

In the past, the Cree made clothing from the furs and skins of animals. Although animal hides were very durable, once the Cree started trading with the Europeans, they also used fabrics they obtained through trading to make clothes.

Women wore dresses that had separate sleeves that could be taken off or put on, depending on the weather. In cold weather, the sleeves were attached with string, leather, or twine. Men typically wore leggings and breechcloths. Breechcloths were long pieces of cloth draped over a belt and worn over the leggings. Both men and women wore their hair long, often in braids tied with leather strips. Men sometimes wore fur or leather caps decorated with feathers.

When the Cree started trading with the Europeans, they exchanged animal skins for fabric, beads, and metal. They used these materials to add colourful decorations to their traditional clothing. As well, many Cree adopted the European style of dress. They began to wear shirts, blouses, and trousers.

Traditionally, each feather in a feather warbonnet had to be earned by an act of bravery.

Today, the Cree celebrate their heritage by wearing traditional clothing at special ceremonies and events. Many craftspeople have learned how to make traditional clothing and have passed the art down to younger generations. Cree people today often combine traditional pieces of clothing with jeans or T-shirts.

The traditional clothing worn by Cree women includes fans, belts, and necklaces.

HAIR ROACHES

Cree men had special headgear that was worn at celebrations and during battle. Porcupine hair roaches were headdresses made from the fur of a porcupine. They ranged in style and colour. Some featured the tail of a deer or a feather. The colours used on the hair roach often represented specific religious beliefs. Today, porcupine hair roaches are worn during dances at celebrations and performances.

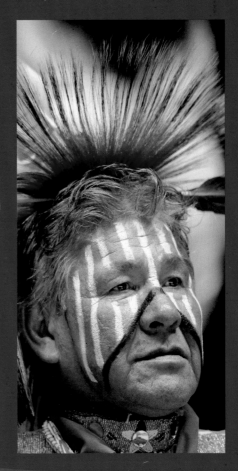

Cree Food

Like many Aboriginal groups, the Cree relied on the land for all their food. Traditionally, the Cree hunted animals such as caribou, deer, moose, and bison. Cree who lived near water also fished. Birds, such as ducks and geese, were an important part of the Cree diet, too.

Animal meat was dried, smoked, or salted to preserve it during the long winter months. The Cree used their dried supplies to make pemmican. Pemmican was made from dried meat, animal fat, and berries or nuts. The mixture was mashed together and dried or stored in containers. People took it on long journeys because it did not spoil.

In addition to meat and fish, the Cree ate nuts and vegetables, such as wild mushrooms and wild turnips. They also ate many kinds of berries. Like meat, the berries were often dried, so they could be stored and eaten throughout the winter.

Bison was the main source of food for the Plains Cree.

RECIPE

Moose Stew

Ingredients:

- 1 kilogram of moose (or beef) in cubes
- 5 teaspoons salt
- 6 cups water
- 5 carrots, sliced or cubed
- 4 stalks of celery, sliced
- 2 cups canned tomatoes
- 2 medium potatoes, cubed
- 1/2 teaspoon savory
- 1 bay leaf
- 1 large onion
- salt and pepper
- cooking oil

Equipment:

- large pot
- measuring spoons

Directions:

1. With an adult's help, brown the meat in a large pot. Add the onions, and cook them until they are almost clear.

2. Add the vegetables, spices, and water.

3. Cover, and simmer for at least one hour.

Tools, Weapons, and Defense

Tools were important to the daily life of the Cree. They were often made from materials the Cree had on hand. Wood and rocks were collected from the area around their camp. The skins and bones of animals they hunted were also used.

The Cree made knives by sharpening stone. The knives were then used to skin animals and cut food. A large stone tool called a maul was used to break and split animal bones, which were then used to make tools and weapons. Sacks made from animal skins were used to store food and hold water. Some supplies, such as dried berries, grains, and meat, were stored in containers made from tree bark.

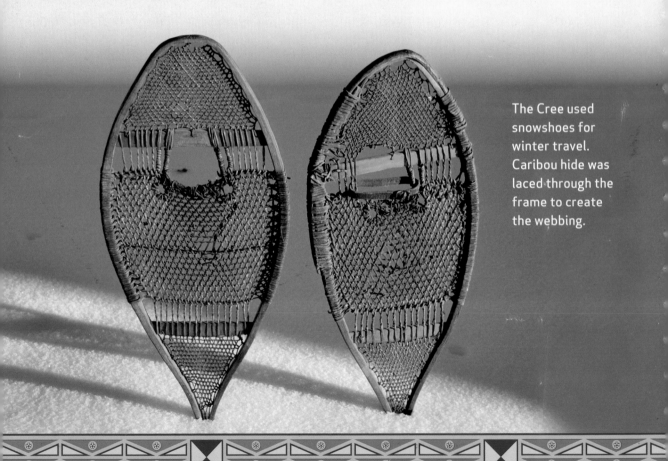

The Cree used snowshoes for winter travel. Caribou hide was laced through the frame to create the webbing.

Utensils, such as spoons, were made from wood, bone, or the horns of moose, deer, or buffalo. Some Cree also used shells as utensils. Dishes were made from carved wood or birchbark.

Before the arrival of Europeans, the Cree used bows and arrows for hunting and warfare. They also used knives, clubs, and spears as weapons.

The Cree depended on dogs and **travois** for transportation before the Europeans introduced horses. Horses soon came to represent power and wealth to the Cree and transformed their way of life.

The Cree used a tool called a crooked knife for hollowing out wood to make canoes, paddles, and spoons.

HUNTING AND DEFENSE

The Cree made **bows** from long pieces of wood, with sections cut out on either end to hold the bow string.

Arrows were made by sharpening the ends of long straight branches.

Arrowheads were made out of **rock, bone,** or **antler**.

A horse was the most valuable gift a Cree could give.

A horse skilled enough for **bison-hunting** was a rare possession for a Cree.

Cree Religion

The Cree had close relationships with the land where they lived, their families, and their ancestors. Each influenced the Cree's **spiritual** beliefs. The Cree believed that all things in nature should be respected. Animals, places, and people all had spirits, and these spirits helped to guide the living.

Animals that were hunted were very highly respected and honoured. It was customary for the Cree to perform ceremonies to ask for blessings from the animals they hunted. They depended on these animals for food, so these **rituals** were very important. The Cree believed that bad luck came to those who did not respect the spirit world.

Shamans were the Cree's religious leaders. They could communicate with the spirit world and ask for blessings. Shamans had the power to heal the sick and speak to the dead.

The Cree often performed rituals before important events, such as the bison hunt.

A number of First Nations peoples, including the Cree, believed in a spirit known as Windigo. The legend of the Windigo varies from group to group. Some Cree believed the Windigo was an evil spirit that tried to harm people. Others believed that the Windigo was a frightening giant that walked the Earth hunting humans. Some thought that the Windigo was a person who had been turned into a Windigo by a spell, a dream, or by being bitten by a Windigo.

The Plains Cree believed that they could tell the future by looking into water. They would do this before hunting or going into battle.

CREE BELIEFS

When someone died, the Cree believed in showing **respect** by **clipping** the **tail** and **mane** of the person's horse.

The Cree believed in a Creator or **Great Spirit** called **Gitche Manitou.**

According to the Cree, thunder comes from the *Thunderbird* flapping its wings.

The Cree believed that the hunted animal, not the hunter, decided the outcome of the hunt.

Ceremonies and Celebrations

The Cree held many celebrations and festivals throughout the year. These celebrations honoured family, friends, and nature. They often marked important events in people's lives. Celebrations gave people a chance to give thanks for their good fortune. They were a time for families and communities to come together.

The Cree also came together to play games of skill and chance throughout the year. Games were not only played for fun. Most games trained agility and dexterity, improving hunting and survival skills.

When Europeans settled in Cree territory, many Cree became **Christians**. Today, some Cree celebrate Christian holidays, such as Christmas. Others combine Christian and Cree traditions.

Many Cree communities are working to preserve their traditions. They often gather to honour their ancestors and practise the traditions of their **elders**. Powwows are special celebrations that include dancing, craft making, and storytelling.

The Walking Out Ceremony is celebrated when a child learns to walk.

CREE GAMES

In lacrosse, players used a pole with a net on the end to toss a ball. Each team tried to score into the other team's goal.

When playing **Toss the Ball,** players stood in a circle and volleyed the ball to each other. If they missed, they were out. The last player left won.

Each player in **Snow Snake** tossed a long stick onto an icy snowbank. The stick that slid the farthest won.

Boys had 4 tries at shooting their arrows as close as possible to the target arrow in the **Shooting Arrow Game.**

Music and Dance

Music has always been an important part of Cree life. It was used to celebrate the lives, the landscape, and the history of the Cree people. Traditionally, music was performed at celebrations to give thanks for a happy event or important time of year. In the past, large groups of people would gather to participate.

One of the most important instruments the Cree used in musical performances and celebrations was the drum. Drums were made from birchbark frames and were covered with deerskins. They were pounded with the player's hand or a mallet to make sound.

Hunting songs were especially important to the Cree. Each hunter had his own songs. The songs held important information, such as where to find certain animals and the best way to catch them. The songs ensured the success of the hunt and therefore the survival of the community.

The drums made by the Cree were only used for special occasions, such as ceremonies and powwows.

CREE SONGS

Singing was an important part of Cree celebrations. The Cree used songs to thank the spirits for their good fortune. They believed that songs brought blessings and healed the sick. Songs were performed at celebrations, festivals, and ceremonies that marked important times in a person's life.

Singers usually performed while they danced or for other dancers. Songs were sung by more than one person, and large groups of people often joined in. Cree songs used repeating notes and sounds, and were often accompanied by drums, bells, and rattles.

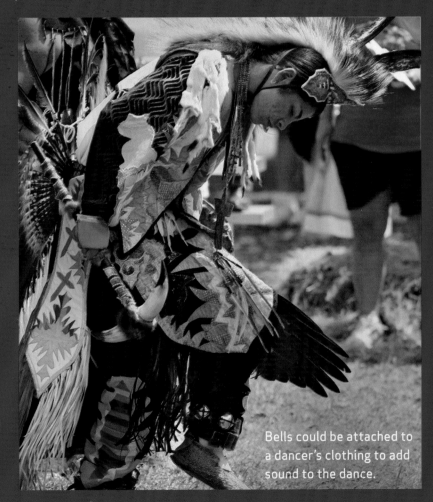

Bells could be attached to a dancer's clothing to add sound to the dance.

Language and Storytelling

The Cree speak different **dialects** from the **Algonquian** language family. There are five main dialects spoken by the Cree. These dialects are influenced by the region in which the people live. Today, more than 80,000 people in Canada have a Cree dialect as their mother tongue.

The Cree use a special alphabet to write their language. Different symbols are used in different positions to represent the 26 letters of the alphabet. Some **historians** believe the Europeans taught the Cree their written language. Others believe the Cree have used some form of written language for hundreds of years.

Schools in areas with a large Cree population teach the Cree language.

Even though Cree can be written, it is mainly an oral language that has been passed down from generation to generation through storytelling. Cree stories were told during celebrations, ceremonies, and for entertainment. They were also used to teach important lessons and the history of the Cree people.

At the First Nations University in Saskatchewan, students can get a Bachelor of Arts degree in Cree.

ORIGIN STORIES

Many of the stories told by the Cree explain their history and origins. The James Bay Cree are just one group that has a story of this nature. The story begins long ago, when the Cree were constantly on the move as they followed herds of animals to supply their food. The people were content hunting and fishing for survival. However, there came the day that they wanted a permanent place to live.

One of the elders contacted the Creator to ask for advice. He was told that a goose would be sent to find the Cree a permanent home. The goose flew to all four corners of the continent. Finally, the goose dropped nine feathers around the James Bay area, in present-day Ontario and Quebec. The Cree have lived there ever since.

Cree Art

The Cree are well known for their beadwork, quilling, carving, and sculptures. Cree artists are inspired by the land around them, the spirits of the animals and people they worship, their history, and their culture.

The Cree decorated clothing and accessories with coloured glass beads. They sewed beads of different colours together to depict flowers, geometric shapes, and other patterns. Ceremonial clothing was decorated with particularly elaborate designs.

The Cree used materials from their natural surroundings, such as wood and stone, for their crafts. They carved tools for daily chores, such as knife handles, but also figures of people and animals, or scenes of daily life. Masks of spirits or animals were carved for celebrations and ceremonies. The Cree also used masks in performances and dances that told stories about Cree history and culture.

Birchbark biting is another traditional craft. It uses a technique similar to making a paper snowflake. Artists traced a rough pattern on the back of a piece of birchbark before folding it into a square with four layers. The artist then bit a pattern into the piece of bark. When the bark was unfolded, it revealed a perfect geometric pattern. In the past, these patterns were used as templates for beading. Today, they are created as works of art in themselves.

Cree beading could be found on everyday clothing, such as leather leggings and moccasins.

QUILLING

Before Europeans introduced glass beads, the Cree used a technique called quilling to decorate many of the items they used in their everyday lives. Quilling was used for jewellery, household items, bags, boxes, and saddles. First, porcupine quills were soaked to make them softer and easier to work with. Next, they were dyed in bright colours. Then, the quills were woven into animal skins or bark.

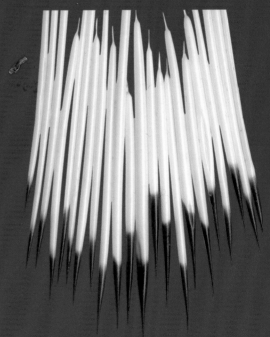

Quilling was a slow and difficult process. Some items took up to a year to decorate.

Body Art

The Cree expressed themselves through their art. They decorated their bodies as a way to express themselves, their heritage, and their beliefs.

Face painting was a common practice among the Cree. Women traditionally painted only their cheeks, while men would cover their entire face. Animal grease was applied to the skin, and then chalky rock or plant substances were ground and rubbed into the area to create different colours. Red, created with a rock called ochre, was very common. Men also painted their faces during battle.

Tattooing was another traditional form of body art. Tattooing was done as part of a religious ceremony. Both men and women had tattoos. These patterns represented a person's relationships with nature, their family, or their community. Tattooing was done with sharp needles and charcoal.

Cree men often covered large parts of their bodies with tattoos.

CONTEMPORARY CREE ART

Allen Sapp is a Cree artist who grew up on the Red Pheasant Reserve in Saskatchewan. As a young man, he started painting what he thought people wanted to see. Fortunately, he met somebody who encouraged him to paint about his heritage instead. When Allen started to paint scenes from his past and the daily life of the Cree, he slowly developed his own unique style. Soon, his work was being exhibited throughout Canada, Great Britain, and the United States. Since then, Allen has received many honours and awards recognizing his contribution to Canadian culture.

Today, face painting is usually only done for ceremonies and celebrations.

STUDYING THE CREES' PAST

Archaeologists use items from the past to learn about different peoples. **Artifacts** left by the Cree and their ancestors help archaeologists determine what life was like hundreds and thousands of years ago.

Pottery, tools, and the remains of camping sites give archaeologists clues to what daily life was like for the early Cree. Archaeologists have found artifacts in Quebec, Alberta, and Saskatchewan that are thousands of years old. These artifacts also help archaeologists understand the migration of the Cree and their ancestors.

Timeline

Archaic Period

5000 B.C.—1000 B.C.

Ancestors of the Cree live throughout Canada and the United States. They survive by hunting deer, elk, bear, and beaver. They also fish and collect berries and nuts.

Woodland Period

1000 B.C.—1000 A.D.

The Cree settle in the wooded areas of what are now Ontario and Quebec. They continue to hunt and fish for survival, but also begin to form settlements. Archaeologists have found pottery from this period.

First European Contact

Early 1600s

French explorers arrive in North America in search of furs. They give the name Cree to the people they meet.

Cree artifacts are displayed at museums throughout Canada. Stone arrowheads, cooking tools, drums, and ceremonial clothing help people to learn more about Cree culture and traditions.

The Cree often used birch wood to make drum hoops. They bent the wood, so the outer side of the wood formed the outer side of the hoop.

The Hudson's Bay Company

1670

The Hudson's Bay Company, a fur-trading business, is established in North America. With the help of the Cree, the company becomes highly successful and leads to the founding of Canada.

The Grand Council of Crees

1970s

The Cree protest against development in their territory. The Grand Council of Crees is formed to help protect the rights of the Cree people in Canada and parts of the United States.

Beginning of a New Era

2002

The Cree of Quebec sign a landmark agreement with the government giving the Cree control over development of their lands.

QUIZ

1 How many people in Canada today have a Cree dialect as their mother tongue?

A. More than 80,000

2 What are the three main groups of the Cree called?

A. The Woods Cree, the Plains Cree, and the Swampy Cree

3 Why did the Plains Cree move so often?

A. To follow the migrating herds of bison, caribou, elk, and moose

4 What were the temporary shelters built by the Plains Cree called?

A. Teepees

5 How did the Cree play an important role in the settlement of Canada?

A. They helped to establish the fur trade.

6 What ingredients were used to make pemmican?

A. Dried meat, animal fat, and berries or nuts

7 Which animal did the Cree use for transportation before they had horses?

A. The dog

8 Who were the religious leaders in Cree society?

A. The shamans

9 How did the Cree decorate their clothing before beads were introduced by Europeans?

A. With quilling

10 Which Cree ceremony took place when a child learned to walk?

A. The Walking Out Ceremony

FURTHER RESOURCES

BOOKS

Enjoy a traditional Cree story with **Mwakwa Talks to the Loon: A Cree Story** by Dale Auger (Heritage House Publishing Company Ltd., 2007).

The Cree language is explored in **Cree: Language of the Plains** by Jean Okimasis (University of Regina Press, 2004).

WEBSITES

To find out more about the Cree and their way of life, visit the following websites. Other reputable websites usually include government sites, educational sites, and online encyclopedias.

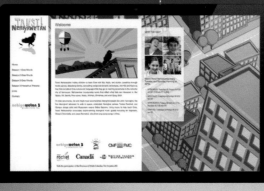

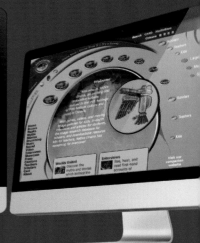

For information on the Cree people and their traditions, visit Land of the People at

www.discovereeyouistchee.ca/cree-culture/traditions.shtml

To learn more about the Cree language, visit Tansi! Nehiyawetan at

www.tansi.tv/creewords/

To find out how to make a Cree drum, visit Native Drums at

www.native-drums.ca/index.php/Drumming/A_Cree_Drum

KEY WORDS

Algonquian: a family of languages spoken by Aboriginal peoples living mainly in central and eastern North America

ancestors: relatives who lived a very long time ago

archaeologists: scientists who study objects from the past to learn about people who lived long ago

artifacts: items, such as tools, made by humans in the past

Christians: people who practise a religion based on the teachings of Jesus Christ

culture: the arts, beliefs, habits, and institutions characteristic of a community, people, or country

dialects: variations of a language that are spoken in certain areas

elders: an older and influential member of a group or community

First Nations: members of Canada's Aboriginal community who are not Inuit or Métis

fur trade: the exchange of furs for European goods

historians: people who study the past

migrated: moved from one place to another

reserves: areas set apart by the federal government for a special purpose, especially for use by an Aboriginal group

rituals: systems or forms of ceremonies

spiritual: sacred or religious

traditions: established beliefs, opinions, and customs

travois: a vehicle made of two poles and an attached platform that is pulled by a dog or other animal

INDEX